THE STORY OF

# JIM HENSON,
## Creator of the Muppets

THE STORY OF

# JIM HENSON,
## Creator of the Muppets

BY STEPHANIE ST. PIERRE

A YEARLING BOOK

## ABOUT THIS BOOK

The events described in this book are true. They have been carefully researched and excerpted from authentic autobiographies, writings, and commentaries. No part of this biography has been fictionalized. To learn more about Jim Henson, ask your librarian to recommend other fine books you might read.

*In memory of Jim Henson
with many thanks for much inspiration*

Published by
Dell Publishing
a division of
Bantam Doubleday Dell Publishing Group, Inc.
666 Fifth Avenue
New York, New York 10103

ISBN: 0-440-40453-3

Published by arrangement with Parachute Press, Inc.
Printed in the United States of America
April 1991
10  9  8  7  6  5  4  3  2  1
OPM

# Contents

# Author's Note

I met Jim Henson when I was eleven years old. In those days he was just my best friend Lisa's dad. He was a little different from the other dads I knew, though. For one thing, he dressed funny. He wore jeans and flowered shirts, and sometimes he even wore a flowered tie. He carried a small leather bag with a long shoulder strap that he called his pouch. It looked a lot more like a purse than a briefcase, which is what most of the other dads carried.

Most dads wore suits and worked in offices. Jim, who had long hair and a beard, wore a suede jacket. Sometimes he wore a leather hat that looked to me a little like a cowboy's. His twinkling blue eyes crinkled up at the corners when he smiled or laughed, which was pretty often.

When Lisa and I went with him to New York City, I had to jog to keep up with his long-legged walk. He was very tall. He was always on his way to a studio or a workshop. But he liked to stop and look at interesting things in shop windows. He was curious about everything.

It wasn't until I'd known Lisa for a while that I realized just what her dad did. He was a puppeteer! Some of the other kids in school thought it was silly. But as *Sesame Street* became more popular, suddenly Mr. Henson wasn't just fun and kind of wacky, he was famous.

I thought that was pretty neat—especially since I was invited to go along to the studio sometimes, where I saw Muppets being made. I not only got to meet some of the puppeteers, but I got to watch them perform while they taped sketches for the show. It was fun and very interesting. Jim would take us out for lunch or ice cream when he had time for a break. On the drive home we talked and giggled and listened to the radio. I never forgot the exciting times I had in New York City with my friend Lisa and her family.

While I was in college, I didn't see the Hensons as often. They were traveling a lot more, and I was busy with school. The Muppets had become even bigger stars. Still, whenever I did see the Hensons they seemed like the same family as ever.

Jim had a wonderful voice, a little like Kermit the Frog's, but richer. He moved his hands when he spoke. They were graceful and expressive and seemed almost to speak for themselves. Of course when he was performing that's exactly what they did! I remember how he used to greet me when I would drop by to visit Lisa. He was always friendly and interested in how things were going for me. He gave me good advice that helped me decide to become a writer and an artist. When I talked about how confusing it was sometimes to grow up and find a career, he really listened.

When Jim Henson died I was very sad. I had looked forward to telling him about how much I loved writing for children. I wanted my own children to have the chance to meet him someday. But as I worked on this book I felt less sad. Jim created so much happiness, it is hard not to feel better just thinking about him. Writing this book is my way of sharing some of what Jim gave me. It's also my way of saying thank you to him.

# A River of Rainbows

It was a rainy day in New York. A crowd of photographers and television news crews stood outside a huge church called the Cathedral of St. John the Divine. A long line of people filed slowly into the church. A mother held her five-year-old by the hand. The little girl snuggled an Ernie doll. A businessman in a dark suit with a bright green tie followed them. Sometimes the photographers saw a famous face in the line. Most of the faces looked sad.

As people removed their raincoats, the cathedral came alive with color. People wore bright blue dresses, pink scarves, yellow jackets and bright green suits—even yellow feathers. As people were ushered into their seats they were given colorful paper butterflies to wave in the air. In no time the church was full. Over *five thousand* people were there to say good-bye to a wonderful man. Big Bird was there, too, along with a lot of other Muppets. Only Kermit was missing.

The air was filled with the smell of thousands of flowers. The colorful clothes and flowers made the church look as if it had been filled by a river of rainbows. The crowd waited. Then the music started. A Dixieland band marched all the way from the back of the cathedral to the front playing music that echoed in the giant space. People began to smile.

Throughout the church hung pictures of Jim Henson, the man these people had come to remember. He had died suddenly only a few days before. It was nice to see his smiling face again. The ceremony in the cathedral was a celebration of his amazing life.

Jim Henson created over two thousand Muppets. He was only fifteen when he started making puppets, and he didn't stop until his death at the age of 53. Kermit the Frog is probably Jim's most famous Muppet. In some ways, Jim and Kermit were very much alike. They were both happy most of the time, and they got along well with people. But Jim created many Muppets besides Kermit, including Ernie, the good-natured joker of Sesame Street, and Rowlf, the piano-playing, wise-cracking dog.

And who can forget rock-and-roller Dr. Teeth; the silly Swedish Chef; grumpy old Waldorf; Guy Smiley, the gameshow host; or Link Hogthrob, the pig in outer space?

Jim was a great puppeteer. He was a creative genius, which means he had a lot of really terrific ideas and could bring them to life in new, exciting ways. And many of those ideas became a reality only because he was also such a good businessman. Jim Henson saw life as a marvelous adventure worthy of his best effort. This is the story of how he gave that effort—and more.

# Down by the Creek

Kermit always said he came from a small swamp in Mississippi. Actually it wasn't a swamp, it was a creek—Deer Creek.

Deer Creek is a wide, deep stream that runs through Leland, Mississippi, the small town where Jim Henson spent his early years. On warm afternoons, Jim often went fishing in Deer Creek with his cousins Will and Stan, and his brother, Paul. They sat on a bridge and dangled their legs over the edge as they fished. Tall green trees grew near the grass-covered banks of the stream. It was a good place to hang around and talk with friends. It was also a nice place to sit alone and daydream.

Sometimes, if it got very cold in the winter, the creek froze over and Jim and his friends went ice-skating. But most years it was too warm for the creek to freeze. On those Christmases, a parade of floats was set adrift on the water. Lights from the houses that lined the creek were reflected in the water, too. It was a very beautiful sight.

Jim was born on September 24, 1936. His full name was James Maury Henson, but he was usually called Jim, or Jimmy. He lived in Leland with his mother, Betty, his father, Paul Sr., and his older brother, Paul Jr. Jim's father worked as an agricultural research biologist—a scientist who studies the different kinds of crops that animals can eat.

While Jim was a young boy he spent his time the way most kids do, going to school and playing. He liked tennis and horseback riding. And of course, he did a lot of fishing in Deer Creek.

Jim was a good student. His best subject was art, and he loved to draw just for the fun of it. He often spent free time drawing funny cartoons and painting. Jim's grandmother, whom he called Dear, was a painter. Jim loved Dear very much and spent a lot of time with her. He enjoyed watching her create beautiful watercolor and oil paintings. Dear helped Jim with his artwork. She was very proud of her grandson's artistic talents. Later, in high school, Jim would make posters for school dances and draw cartoons for the school newspaper.

When he wasn't busy sketching or painting, Jim liked to take part in school plays. Even though he often felt shy, Jim loved making people laugh. He liked having an audience. He was the kind of kid who couldn't help goofing around whenever somebody took a picture. Maybe it was because he and his brother, Paul, spent a lot of time joking around. Paul was a fun older brother. Sometimes he made Jim laugh by juggling for him.

Jim's uncle Jinx was also very funny and one of Jim's favorite people. Uncle Jinx was a minister. He had a serious side and taught Jim about how it was important to do good deeds. But he also told really good jokes and funny stories. Uncle Jinx's son Stan was one of Jim's very best friends. The whole family of aunts and uncles and cousins lived nearby. They came to visit often. They were a close, happy family. After church in the morning they often spent Sunday afternoons playing croquet. Jim was a good croquet player and loved the game. Jim wasn't very athletic, but he *was* competitive—he loved to win. Jim won often when he played croquet with his family.

Jim also loved to read and go to the movies. "I loved all the Oz books," Jim recalled when he was older. "*The Wizard of Oz* is still one of my favorite movies. It was the first movie I ever saw." It's easy to imagine Jim lying by the creek on a sunny summer day, daydreaming and reading about fantastic places.

When they weren't playing outside, Jim and Paul spent a lot of time listening to the radio. In those days there was no television. "Early radio drama was an important part of my childhood," Jim once said. "I'd go home at four-thirty or five in the afternoon to hear shows like *The Green Hornet, The Shadow,* and *Red Ryder* . . . and of course I loved the comedians." *The Green Hornet* was a show about a superhero; *The Shadow* was a mystery series; *Red Ryder* was a cowboy adventure.

Another radio show that Jim liked featured Edgar Bergen, a ventriloquist, and his dummies Charlie McCarthy and Mortimer Snerd. A ventriloquist is a kind of puppeteer who can speak his puppet's part without moving his own mouth, so it seems as if the puppet is *really* doing the talking. A ventriloquist often uses a dummy, a big doll with a mouth that opens and shuts when the ventriloquist moves a lever in the dummy's back. When Edgar Bergen performed his radio show, a live audience at the radio studio watched him. Sitting in his living room, Jim couldn't *see* Edgar Bergen or his dummies—he could only hear them. But the dummies seemed like real people to Jim. Later when he was working as a puppeteer, Jim wanted to make his own puppets come to life that way.

Leland was a nice town to grow up in. Jim remembered his happy early days there for the rest of his life. Many of the small-town scenes that appeared in the Muppets' movies and television shows came from Jim's memories of that time. But, as wonderful as it was, the Hensons didn't stay in Leland. When Jim was in fifth grade his father got a new job. The family packed up, said good-bye to Deer Creek, and moved to a new home in a place called Hyattsville, Maryland.

# Puppets and Television

Moving was a big change for Jim, but he was a happy boy and soon got used to his new home. Hyattsville is a suburb of Washington, D.C. It is also something of a college town because it is close to the University of Maryland. Hyattsville was about twice the size of Leland, but it was still a comfortable, quiet place to live. And best of all, it was the same town where Jim's grandparents, Dear and Pop, lived.

It wasn't long after he moved to Maryland that something important happened to Jim. He discovered television!

Television officially had begun broadcasting in the United States at the 1939 World's Fair. Franklin Roosevelt, the President at the time, made a speech. But back then only a few people had television sets. It wasn't until the early 1950's that most people owned their own TV's.

Jim was determined to have a TV set—even after his parents refused to buy one! "I was probably about thirteen or fourteen [before] we got our first television set," Jim once said. "I thought it was incredible. It's amazing to see a live picture that comes to you from somewhere else. I've always been in love with television." These days, television seems very ordinary to most of us. But Jim never stopped being amazed by it.

As a teenager, Jim watched a lot of television. By the 1950's, television was broadcasting all kinds of different shows, including mysteries and adventure shows as well as shows with cowboys and superheroes. There were also several shows with puppets in them.

One of the shows Jim liked was called *Kukla, Fran & Ollie*. Kukla, a clown, and Ollie, a dragon, were hand puppets performed by a puppeteer named Burr Tillstrom. Fran Allison was a real woman who stood next to the puppet stage and spoke with the puppets. Burr Tillstrom made up the show as he went along. Burr was a talented puppeteer—his puppets were lively and funny. Many children watched the show and loved it.

Another show featured Bil and Cora Baird, puppeteers who worked with marionettes. Marionettes are usually made out of wood or some other stiff material. Puppeteers make them move by pulling strings or wires attached to the arms, legs, and bodies of the marionettes. The jerky motions marionettes make are fun to watch. The Bairds were very popular. They performed with their marionettes live in theaters as well as on television.

Jim loved TV so much that he decided he wanted to work at a television station. By listening to the radio and watching TV Jim had learned a lot about storytelling, comedy, and performing. But he hadn't yet had an opportunity to work with puppets. So just how *did* he become a puppeteer?

Jim's interest in puppets began when he joined his high school puppet club. And Jim's very first job involved puppets, although he didn't plan it that way. "As soon as I was old enough to get a job," Jim once told a reporter, "I went out and approached all the small studios in Washington to apply for work." Finally, in the summer of 1954, when Jim was only seventeen, he got his first break.

When Jim heard that the local TV station, WTOP, was looking for a puppeteer, he and a friend built a few simple hand puppets. He auditioned and landed his first job in TV as a puppeteer for a children's show called the *Junior Good Morning Show*. His puppets were a French rat named Pierre and a couple of cowboys named Longhorn and Shorthorn. Jim did a great job, but the show was canceled after only three weeks. But Jim didn't have much time to be upset. Soon he found another job helping out with a cartoon show on the local NBC station, WRC-TV.

Jim had grown into a tall, thin young man. Sometimes he could be very shy. He was self-conscious about his acne, so he grew a beard to cover the scars on his face. But when he was performing, or just clowning around, Jim could overcome his shyness.

By the time he graduated from high school, Jim had built his own puppets and began performing. But he didn't take puppetry very seriously. He wanted to get a job as a commercial artist. A commercial artist does artwork in many different areas, such as drawings for advertisements, or cartoons for newspapers and magazines. Still, Jim hoped that somehow he would find a way to work in television. As for puppets, they were just kid stuff. When the time was right, Jim thought he would leave them behind and begin a serious career.

**Jim Henson with some of the Muppets he created and performed, Dr. Teeth and the Swedish Chef (left to right, back row), Rowlf the Dog, Kermit the Frog, and Mr. Waldorf (front row). (1977)**

**Kermit the Frog addresses the Harvard University Class of 1982 during Senior Week activities. Jim's daughter Lisa was a Harvard student.**

**Jane Henson looks for a place to store a Muppet called Big V. (1965)**

**Jim hugs a fraggle from his television show *Fraggle Rock*. (1983)**

Jim talks to young Muppet fans at the Museum of Science and Industry in Chicago. Miss Piggy, Kermit, and Big Bird were part of a "Muppets and Friends" exhibition there. (1983)

The 120 episodes of *The Muppet Show* brought Jim Henson recognition as an entertainer of adults as well as children. (1984)

The marriage of Kermit and Miss Piggy takes place in the third Muppet movie, *The Muppets Take Manhattan*, released in 1984.

Frank Oz performs Miss Piggy while Jim Henson performs Kermit the Frog during the filming of *The Muppets Take Manhattan* in New York City's Central Park.

**Kermit the Frog and Miss Piggy visit Moscow's Red Square.
(1988)**

**Big Bird sings "It's Not Easy Being Green" during the
memorial service for Jim Henson at Cathedral of St. John
the Divine in New York. (1990)**

Jim visits Ronald McDonald House in New York City, a home away from home for families of children receiving treatment at nearby hospitals. (1988)

Muppeteers pay tribute to Jim Henson at the end of his memorial service. The Muppets sway back and forth, singing a medley of children's songs. (1990)

# On the Air

In the fall of 1954, Jim began college at the University of Maryland in nearby College Park, where he studied acting, stagecraft, and scene design. He continued to paint and draw, since his goal was to become a commercial artist. Because of university policy, Jim had to enroll in the home economics department to earn a degree in commercial art! In those days, home ec, as it was called, consisted mainly of classes where women learned about sewing and cooking and housekeeping. Very few men took home ec courses. People acted shocked when Jim told them he was a home economics major. Jim, who always liked to surprise people, thought their reaction was very funny.

Even though he was a full-time college student, Jim still worked at WRC-TV. The money he earned helped pay for his college tuition. He did some puppetry and some cartoon drawing as well. Then, in May of 1955, at the end of his freshman year, Jim was offered a truly wonderful opportunity.

WRC-TV offered him his *very own* show! It was really two very short shows. Jim was given two five-minute time slots, one after the evening news at 6:25 p.m. and the other after the late night news at 11:25. These were good times for Jim's show because lots of people tuned in at these times. Jim called the show *Sam and Friends*. Perhaps he was able to work at such a demanding job while he was also a full-time student because he had so much fun doing it. It wasn't just work—it was play, too. As Jim said, "The show was on so late that nobody attached much importance to it, so we were able to do almost anything we wanted to."

*Sam and Friends* was a program meant for adults. It starred Sam, a funny-looking bald puppet with big eyes and a round nose. Jim had fun creating all kinds of wild characters from his imagination—a talking skull named Yorick, weird monsters that ate anything they could fit in their mouths, goofy-looking characters with huge eyes and funny hats. Some of the other characters on the show looked a little like the Muppets that would appear years later in *Sesame Street* and *The Muppet Show*.

One of the puppets—a creature named Kermit—would one day become a very famous frog. Jim made the very first Kermit using green fabric from one of his mother's old coats for the puppet's body. A Ping-Pong ball cut in half became eyes. At the beginning Kermit didn't even look much like a frog! "He was much more lizardlike," Jim said. "People would say, 'Oh, you've got a frog,' and I'd say, 'No, it's just a creature.' " But over the years Kermit began to look more and more like a frog. While trying to think of a name for the new puppet, Jim had remembered a childhood friend and decided on Kermit.

The amazing thing about *Sam and Friends* was that Jim Henson created a whole new kind of puppet for television. On television the puppets were viewed close up, so for the first time, a puppet's face became really important. Jim Henson realized this. By making his puppets out of soft flexible materials, he changed the way a puppet's face looked as he carefully moved his hand around inside the puppet's head—a bit like a sock puppet, only better.

Jim also began to use puppets without a traditional puppet stage. Puppets performing on a stage are meant to be seen from a distance, so their movements have to be large and exaggerated. Other puppeteers had continued to use stages when they performed with their puppets on television. By getting rid of the puppet stage, Jim was able to create a space for the puppet that seemed more natural and free.

The puppets acted out their scenes on a set in full view of the TV cameras. The set was built high up. Jim had to hold the puppets over his head while he worked so he wouldn't be seen by the cameras. As he worked, Jim looked into a monitor (a small TV), which let him see the puppets exactly as they appeared to the TV viewer. He was his own audience. This helped Jim to make the puppet's movements seem even more realistic. Jim Henson was doing something really incredible—his puppets were coming to life!

Jim named his new creatures Muppets. When asked how he had come up with the term, Jim said the word muppet was a combination of marionette and puppet because Muppets were worked by hand (like puppets), as well as with wires and strings to move arms and legs (like marionettes.) The explanation made sense, but many years later Jim admitted that he had made up the name Muppets because he liked the sound of it—it just seemed to fit the creatures he had created.

On *Sam and Friends* the Muppets often did strange things. At first none of them had voices, so instead of talking, they acted out funny scenes to music. They danced or chased each other, or gobbled each other up. Jim once said of the show, "We very often would take a song and do strange things to it . . . that nobody could quite understand . . . I always enjoyed doing those!"

From the very beginning, music was a big part of the Muppets. Jim never called himself a musician, but he had a special talent for choosing the best music for the Muppets' zany antics. With the help of music the Muppets could make an audience laugh at all sorts of things, weird things, silly things, scary things—like ugly creatures who acted sweet and kind, singing frogs, and monsters who ate everything in sight.

Jim's opportunities during his college years were clouded by a terrible tragedy. Jim's older brother, Paul, was killed in a car accident. Paul, who was engaged to be married, was only 22 years old. Jim never stopped missing his brother. In fact, for the rest of his life, Jim remained friendly with his brother's fiancée,

Julie. He often commented on how he missed his brother—that no one could ever take his place.

How many college students actually have their own TV show? *Sam and Friends* gave Jim a chance to use his creative skills to design puppets and stage sets. The show, like the classes he took in college, was a way for Jim to learn and grow as an artist. But as time went on, Jim decided he needed help with *Sam and Friends*. He got it from a friend he met in a college puppetry class. His new partner was a fellow student named Jane Nebel. When she and Jim began working together, they had no idea that their partnership would last a very long time.

# Partners

Jane Nebel was a student of fine arts education. She and Jim were both interested in art as well as puppetry. They enjoyed talking about painting and going to art exhibits together. They talked about how their art was and how it could be used to tell people about new ideas. They not only had fun together but admired each other's talents.

Jane was a great help to Jim with *Sam and Friends*. Like Jim, Jane had a wonderful, zany sense of humor and was a careful craftsperson. As they worked happily together creating many more wonderful creatures, they became good friends. And they made a terrific team.

In 1956 Jane and Jim were invited to perform their Muppet act on the *Tonight* show with Steve Allen. Until then only people in and near Washington, D.C., had seen *Sam and Friends*, but the *Tonight* show was broadcast all over the country. It was an exciting break. Jim worked

Kermit, who wore a blond wig and sang the song "I've Grown Accustomed to Your Face." Jane worked a purple monster called Yorick. As Kermit sang, the monster began to eat the happy face mask he was wearing. Once the monster finished, he went after Kermit and tried to gobble him up, too. (Almost ten years later, the gobbling creature would become Cookie Monster.) "In the early days of the Muppets we had two endings," Jim said. "Either one creature ate the other or both of them blew up. So I've always been particular to things eating other things." Their *Tonight* show appearance was a great success!

In 1957 the Muppets were hired to make TV commercials for a company called Wilkins Coffee. Jim created all the commercials. He was writing, directing, and performing. He was also beginning to learn about business as well as puppetry. In fact, that year Jim and Jane legally became business partners.

The eight-second-long coffee commercials (160 of them in all!) were very funny. At first, the Muppets ate each other up or blew each other up. Then Jim began making up voices for them. Jim learned to use his voice in different ways for his many characters. Jane continued to help *perform* puppets, while Jim did the voices.

So much was happening for Jim, Jane, and the Muppets. All of their hard work was beginning to pay off. Between their pay from *Sam and Friends* and from the coffee commercials, Jim and Jane were beginning to make quite a lot of money for college students. When Jim graduated from college in 1958 he was able to buy a fancy old car called a Rolls Royce to drive to his graduation.

Jim had always loved fancy cars. But he found other ways to spend his money as well. He planned a summer trip to Europe. Before he left, Jim decided that he should begin thinking about a new career when he got home. He thought about becoming a painter, or maybe a filmmaker. Puppetry had been fun and he had even made money at it. But, as he said, "All the time I was in school I didn't take puppetry seriously. I mean, it didn't seem to be the sort of thing a grown man works at for a living."

Even so, while he was in Europe, Jim couldn't help looking for puppeteers wherever he went. In the United States, Jim had felt discouraged because people thought of puppets

41

only as children's entertainment. They didn't care about the artistic effort that went into building puppets and performing them.

In Europe, Jim discovered that things were different. "They were very serious about their work," said Jim of the European puppeteers he met. "I thought what they were doing was really interesting." In Europe puppeteers were considered artists, and their puppets were carefully and beautifully made. They worked at their craft with enthusiasm, and their audiences were made up of people of all ages. When Jim returned home in the autumn, he decided to make puppeteering his career after all. Soon he was back at work with Jane on *Sam and Friends*—but with a new excitement. Puppeteering now felt like a *real* job.

1959 was a very important year for Jim and Jane. They won an Emmy Award for the Best Local Entertainment Program. Winning the Emmy was a great achievement, and everyone working on *Sam and Friends* was very proud and excited. Together Jim and Jane had created a truly unique and important program. They had begun to change the way people thought of puppets.

That same year, Jim and Jane decided to

get married. Jane is an artistic, intelligent, gentle woman. She and Jim worked well together, and they brought out the best in each other. They were happy together. It was a good time for them. They had managed to build a wonderful business together, and now they wanted to build a home and a family.

# A Creative Family

In 1960 Jim and Jane had their first child, a girl they named Lisa. Jane still spent time performing and she remained Jim's business partner. In 1961 another daughter, Cheryl, was born. Jane did less performing then. That year Jim also began to build another sort of family— the people who would help the Muppets grow and become a huge success.

One of the first people to join the Muppet family was a man named Bernie Brillstein, who worked as Jim's agent. An agent helps an artist, writer, or performer to find work, negotiate contracts, and schedule appearances. Jim met Bernie late in 1961 thanks to Burr Tillstrom, the puppeteer of *Kukla, Fran & Ollie*. Burr Tillstrom wanted to help Jim with his career, so he asked Bernie Brillstein to talk to Jim.

Mr. Brillstein told a reporter about his first meeting with Jim. Jim had arrived at Mr. Brillstein's office wearing his usual unusual outfit. "I didn't want to see him," Brillstein said. As he described him, Jim looked like a "young Abe Lincoln wearing some kind of hippie arts-and-craft clothes." But before Brillstein had a chance to send Jim away, an incredible thing happened. "Just then my boss called and said, 'Have you ever heard of Jim Henson and the Muppets?'" Bernie Brillstein was glad to be able to say that Jim happened to be sitting in his office at that very moment!

Jim knew that finding a good agent was very important for his business. Bernie Brillstein and Jim Henson decided to work together and shook hands to seal their agreement. They never signed a contract, but they worked together happily for the next thirty years. This sort of arrangement is very unusual. In show business few people are willing to work together without a written contract. Jim felt that his word and the word of the person he was doing business with were enough in some cases. He was willing to trust people to be fair and honest. And he was fair and honest with them in return.

The final season for *Sam and Friends* was 1961. The Muppets were now appearing as "guests" on many different shows as well as doing occasional commercials. They appeared on the *Ed Sullivan Show*. They were on *The Today Show* often. Jim needed to find more puppeteers to work with the Muppets. He needed to meet more people who were interested in doing the same kind of work that he was. Soon he and Jane would move to New York City, where they were more likely to meet other performers.

As he became more serious about puppetry, Jim got involved in Puppeteers of America, a national organization for puppeteers. In fact, he even served as their president for a couple of years. During this time he became friendly with three famous puppeteers who were important to him: Burr Tillstrom, Bil Baird, and a marionettist named Rufus Rose, who was the puppeteer for a popular 1950's TV show called *Howdy Doody*.

Each year the Puppeteers of America held a convention at which puppeteers from all over the country had a chance to meet. At these conventions there was lots of talking and performing. Everyone wanted to learn more about what other puppeteers in the United States were doing.

At the National Puppet Convention in

1961, Jim met two people who would be especially important to the Muppets: Jerry Juhl and Frank Oz. Jerry started working with Jim right away, but Frank, who was performing at the convention with his father, a talented traditional puppeteer, was only sixteen and still in high school. Frank wouldn't be ready to join the Muppets for a few more years. But Jim kept in touch with him, realizing that one day Frank would be a good addition to the Muppet family.

During this time Jim was experimenting with his Muppets, trying to get them to seem more lifelike. Jim and the people he worked with discovered a new way of making them talk. Instead of moving the Muppets' mouths as often as human mouths do while talking, the Muppets would open and shut their mouths only on the most important parts of a word. This way, they seemed to be talking normally, instead of their mouths flapping open and shut too quickly. But it wasn't an easy thing for a puppeteer to master.

"The mechanics of puppeteering is like playing a musical instrument," Jim explained. "It's something that you have to do long enough so that it becomes absolutely how you think. You have to think through your arm or your hand." The puppeteers had to practice hard to be able to use the new technique. And not everyone could learn to be a great Muppet performer.

To get an idea of just how difficult being a Muppet performer is, try this simple exercise. First, hold one arm straight up over your head. Let your hand drop as you bend your wrist. Now make your hand "talk" by tapping your top fingers against your thumb. That isn't too hard. Try it again, and this time keep your thumb stiff. Gently curve your top fingers, holding them together tight. Next tap your thumb against your top fingers *without letting them move*. Now that's hard! It doesn't take long before your arm begins to feel sore and your fingers ache. Imagine doing that for hours on end, holding the weight of a heavy puppet high up over your head. As Jim put it, "The only way the magic works is by hard work."

The puppets themselves were changing, too. They became more complicated to perform. Some were still simple hand puppets. Others required a team of puppeteers—one puppeteer to work the mouth and right arm, and a second or even a third puppeteer to work the left arm and legs, or whatever other parts a creature might have. It could get pretty crowded under the stage with all those puppeteers crowded into such a small place. Between working the puppets and trying to watch everything on the TV monitor, the puppeteers often turned into one giant puppeteer pretzel!

As the Henson family grew, so did the Muppet family. By 1963 Frank Oz had graduated from college and had come to join the company. Jerry Juhl switched from performing to writing. And a friend named Don Sahlin became the chief puppet builder. Jim had seen plenty of Don's work—for many years Don had worked with Burr Tillstrom. Jim called Don a "master puppet builder."

Don Sahlin improved the Muppets by redesigning them to look a little bit alike, as if they were all related to one another. Each Muppet was still unique, but now they all had big saucer-shaped mouths. Their eyes and noses grew large and were often round.

Now Jim and Jane had three families. A family with children. A family of friends working together. And a growing family of Muppets!

# How They Got to Sesame Street

One of the first Muppets Don Sahlin built was a floppy-eared, piano-playing dog named Rowlf. Rowlf, performed by Jim, was the Muppets' first big star. From 1963 to 1966 Rowlf appeared on the *Jimmy Dean Show*, a variety series with lots of different sketches. Jimmy Dean was a country and western singer and performer popular in the 1950's and 60's. Famous stars would appear on the show to sing or act. Each week Jimmy would sing a song with Rowlf the dog as his piano player. Jimmy treated Rowlf as if he were a person. Rowlf made jokes and chatted with the singer in a gruff, gravelly voice. Sometimes Rowlf even sang a song.

Besides the *Jimmy Dean Show* the Muppets were featured once a month on the *Ed Sullivan Show*, a very important and famous show for new talent. They were guests on many other variety shows. So much was going on that things got pretty hectic. One night the Muppets appeared on *The Perry Como Show*. It was Christmastime. The Muppets performed a musical number with reindeer on *Ed Sullivan*. After the show was over, Kermit Love, the man who had built the reindeer, told Jim that they had forgotten to put ears on the animals! He was worried that people would notice. But Jim wasn't worried—he just said that it was the horns that made the animals look like reindeer. And it was true. The performers did such a good job, they made the audience believe that the Muppets were "real."

At this point, the Muppets were also still doing commercials. But as busy as he was with Muppets, Jim had other projects in the works.

In 1964 he made a ten-minute film called *Timepiece*. In the film all sorts of pictures flash across the screen. There are scenes of Jim dressed in a tuxedo hopping on a pogo stick through a traffic jam. There is also a funny ending where a very tiny Jim is flushed down a toilet! It's a crazy but wonderful movie. In 1965 *Timepiece* was nominated for an Academy Award. Jim made two other unusual films in the sixties. They were called *Youth '68* and *The Cube*.

At home, the Henson family continued to grow. Brian was born in 1963, John in 1965.

As the 1960's drew to a close the Muppets were beginning to be well known by a large audience. Now that the puppeteers and writers and puppet builders worked so well together, the Muppets needed someplace new to show off their work.

Jim had been trying to sell ideas for family shows to different television networks and production companies, but so far nothing had come of it. Around this time Jim met a man named Jon Stone, a writer and producer for children's television. Jim also met a talented musical director and composer name Joe Raposo. The first project Jon, Jim and Joe worked on together was a series pilot called *Hey Cinderella*. It was a funny story inspired by the famous fairy tale. They also made Muppet versions of *The Frog Prince* and *The Brementown Musicians*. Though the pilot was terrific, the network unfortunately decided at the last minute not to make the series. But next Jon Stone called on Jim to help create a new educational program for preschool children called *Sesame Street*.

Joan Ganz Cooney, the person in charge of creating *Sesame Street* for The Children's Television Workshop, wanted to create a television program that would entertain children while teaching them the alphabet and how to count. The show was an effort to give poor children whose parents couldn't afford nursery school the chance to learn basic skills. Mrs. Cooney had been a fan of the Muppets, and she was sure that they could help her program become successful. But no one really had any idea *how* successful. On November 11, 1969, *Sesame Street* aired on television for the first time—and the show became an overnight sensation.

Jim once said, "I guess *Sesame Street* was an important point in my career, because it directed all of my energies into the Muppets." Along with Jim, Jon Stone and the rest of the Muppet team had spent a lot of time thinking about the Muppets they would create for *Sesame Street*. They had decided to invent a special character that children could really relate to. "We wanted to create a character the child could live through," Jim said.

Big Bird's sweet, curious character grew from that simple idea. Big Bird was one of Jim's more innovative Muppets. The eight-foot, two-inch tall bird wasn't performed like any puppet that had come before—Carroll Spinney, the puppeteer who performed Big Bird, was actually inside him! The costume got so hot inside that Big Bird had to be built with his own fan inside. He also had a TV monitor in his costume. Later, other Muppets, such as Mr. Snuffleupagus and Barkley the Dog, were built the same way.

Did you ever wonder why Big Bird is *so* big? It's because Kermit Love originally built Big Bird for Jim, who was a very tall man. When the costume was finished, Jim tried it on. But Kermit Love told Jim that he wasn't really walking like a bird is supposed to. Jim thought about it for a few minutes and realized he wasn't ever going to do it right—walking like a bird just wasn't his style of performing. So Jim hired Carroll Spinney to play the part, but the costume was so big that Carroll had to wear shoes with four-inch high lifts in them! As expected, everyone fell in love with Big Bird.

Jim wanted the Muppets to express an attitude toward life like his own. "As a parent around your children, you behave a certain way," Jim said. "You do positive things that you want them to reflect in their own lives. I feel that I'm a positive person. I think life is basically good. People are basically good. That's the message I would like to express through the Muppets." Like real boys and girls, though, the Muppets had good and bad characteristics. But no Muppets character was ever *really* bad—at worst a Muppet was just a bit mischievous.

Ernie, for example, is a funny guy who loves to play jokes on his best buddy, Bert. The relationship between Ernie and Bert was similar to the real-life friendship between Jim, who performed Ernie, and Frank Oz, who performed Bert. Frank also performed Cookie Monster and Grover, among others.

"Without Jim," said Frank once, "I'm a pretty serious person at times. He was always the leader, but he allowed us to play. We had so much fun." Jim, on the other hand, always thought *Frank* was the funnier one of the two. Jim was a good boss because even when his employees were working hard to get their jobs done, he managed to help them have a good time. Because the people who worked with Jim so often enjoyed themselves, they found it to be a unique and wonderful experience.

Being a puppeteer is a fun job, but it can also be very hard physical work. Muppets are sometimes heavy and difficult to move. The puppeteers have to crouch under the stage and crane their necks to keep an eye on the monitor to see how their puppets look on-screen. Sometimes a puppeteer might not be in the right mood to play a certain character. Jon Stone remembers that Jim didn't like performing Guy Smiley, the loud-mouthed gameshow host. "The voice was so hard on him," Jon said. "The same is true of Frank and Cookie Monster."

Besides Ernie, Guy Smiley, and others, Jim performed his favorite Muppet, Kermit, on *Sesame Street*. As Kermit's character developed, it seemed as if he and Jim had more and more in common. Jim said that Kermit was a little "snarkier"—wiser, tougher, and more explosive. When Jim and Kermit appeared on the *Tonight* show, Jim thought that his own performance was boring, but that Kermit had been really funny. Jim was much shyer and quieter than Kermit. Kermit was also a better singer and got to do some of the best musical numbers on *Sesame Street*.

Music was an important part of the show, since it had always been part of the Muppet act. Joe Raposo and Jeff Moss were two of the people who wrote songs and music for the Muppets. The Muppets made records of their *Sesame Street* songs. Their first hit record was

Ernie's version of "Rubber Duckie." Many of the songs became very popular, but one became extra special for Kermit.

This song, "It's Not Easy Being Green," is about how being green may seem very ordinary and unexciting but is really wonderful and amazing. It's a perfect example of how Jim felt each one of us should appreciate our own special qualities.

Children loved *Sesame Street,* and so did their parents! Why did adults like these puppets so much, anyway? "There is a child in everybody," Jim once explained. "We all remember what it's like to meet an unknown situation for the first time and not have any idea how to face it. All of that is still in us."

Only a year after *Sesame Street* went on the air, Big Bird appeared on the cover of *Time* magazine. Soon *Sesame Street* was being produced in dozens of languages, in countries all over the world. The Muppets were now officially stars!

# HA! HI! HO!

Jim Henson's company continued to grow. He was a careful businessman who always made sure he had the very best people working with him. But the whimsy and imagination that was such a big part of the Muppet characters also appeared in Jim's way of doing business. For one thing he named his company HA!—short for Henson Associates. There was also a part of the company called HI!—Henson International. And HO!—Henson Organization.

Jim spent a lot of money on good materials to make his Muppets, props, and sets. He not only needed to pay the writers, puppeteers, and puppet builders, but he also wanted to experiment with new ways of making and using puppets. Jim needed to find ways for the Muppets to make enough money so that he could pay all his expenses. And he did.

One of the things the Muppets did to make money was make business meeting films. These films were fun and silly. They were shown during breaks at meetings for salesmen and managers. They featured Muppet salesmen who talked about actual business topics, but with a bit of Muppet silliness thrown in. Business became really fun when the Muppets took charge!

Despite his hectic schedule, Jim still managed to spend time with his large family. In 1970 the Hensons' fifth and youngest child, Heather, was born. Jane often brought the children and their friends to the studio to watch the Muppets at work. Sometimes the Henson children even got into the act by appearing on *Sesame Street* segments.

All the children were encouraged to be creative. Jim and his eldest daughter, Lisa, built a wonderful dollhouse together. When Lisa and a friend were working on the dollhouse one day at the studio, Jim dropped by to introduce them to the superstar Cher! She had come to the studio with her own daughter, Chastity, who was taping a segment for *Sesame Street*.

The studio was like a strange new world. It was full of worktables with Muppets-in-progress: foam faces and feathers sat next to weird eyeballs, piles of noses, and patches of fur. Drawings pinned to the walls showed the puppet builders what to do as they worked on new creatures. Drawings weren't the only inspiration for Muppets, however. Sometimes Jim would come into the studio while the puppet builders were working and slip a partly finished Muppet on his hand. The staff would watch as Jim brought a magical new quality to the Muppet by experimenting with it. The best Muppets grew out of puppeteers and puppet builders working together.

The regular cast of Muppet characters were kept in their own special, carefully labeled drawers when not in use. It was strange to open a drawer and see a lifeless Oscar the Grouch or Bert staring out of it. There were also drawers full of eyes, noses, eyebrows, horns, feathers, hats, wigs, fur, and other bits and pieces of stuff that could be attached to all-purpose Muppet bodies.

The puppeteers, designers, and builders all worked closely together. They might spend whole days trying to find a way to build a puppet so that his cheeks would puff out just right when he played the saxophone. Jim was always around to give suggestions and encouragement. He was very concerned with details, and he became excited when he discovered something new—a material that would make a monster look especially strange, or a special kind of eyeball that would make a Muppet seem more real. For example, the first Ernie head was made from a large Nerf ball. And his eyes were made from plastic spoons! Jim never stopped looking for ways to make the Muppets more interesting, or to make a new and different kind of Muppet. He was rewarded for all his efforts in 1974, when the Sesame Street Muppets won an Emmy Award for Outstanding Achievement in Children's Programming.

By the mid-1970's Jim was ready to bring the Muppets to prime-time network television in a new program, to be called *The Muppet Show,* that would entertain adults as well as children. Unfortunately, the three major TV networks— ABC, NBC, and CBS—all turned down Jim's idea. They still thought that Muppets were only for kids, especially since *Sesame Street* had been so successful. It looked as if *The Muppet Show* might never become a reality.

Although Jim was happy that *Sesame Street* was a big success, he was frustrated to find himself back where he had started at the beginning of his career. Once again he was trying to convince people that puppets weren't just for children. But in 1975 Jim did manage to find a place for his "grown-up" Muppets on a new late-night comedy show called *Saturday Night Live*.

The Muppets created for *Saturday Night Live* were very strange. (Similar characters reappeared later as the evil Skeksis in Jim's film *The Dark Crystal*.) These scary Muppets acted out the weirder side of Jim Henson's sense of humor—there were lots of explosions, the creatures burped, and they pulled off their arms or eyeballs. They were funny, but they were also pretty gross.

Meanwhile, Jim didn't give up on *The Muppet Show*. Early in 1976, Jim finally found someone who was willing to supply the money and the means to get *The Muppet Show* off the ground. That person was a wealthy English businessman, Lord Grade.

Lord Grade was another person with whom Jim did business on the basis of a handshake. Lord Grade had only one condition for Jim: the show had to be produced in England. And so it was.

# A Frog with a Dream

The Muppets had been thinking about moving for a while, though they never expected to move quite so far. So Jim kept his offices in New York City open and set up a second studio especially for *The Muppet Show* in London. He also bought a house there so that his family could join him during the six months each year he would be in England.

The basic idea of *The Muppet Show* was that Kermit, Miss Piggy, Gonzo, Fozzie, and a bunch of other Muppets were trying to put on a show in a small theater with a different guest star each week.

Jim didn't plan for Kermit to be the show's central character, but after much trial and error, Kermit worked best. After twenty years as a minor player, Kermit became a star. He was the perfect character to calm the chaos the rest of the Muppets created on the show. In the same way, Jim was always calmly working his way through things no matter how crazy they got.

The cast of *The Muppet Show* included dozens of new characters as well as some old ones. Of course Jim performed Kermit the Frog and another regular, Rowlf the Dog. Jim's new characters included Link Hogthrob, the intrepid captain of Pigs in Space; the Swedish Chef; Dr. Teeth, the grizzly rock and roller; and Waldorf, the sour old man who complained and taunted from the audience.

Waldorf was joined by another crabby character, Stadtler, who was performed by Richard Hunt, a new recruit. Richard also worked Scooter, the show's intellectual, and Janice, a California surfer-girl band member. Richard's character Beaker was the terrified assistant of Bunsen Honeydew, a quiet mad scientist performed by another new puppeteer, Dave Goelz. Dave also performed Gonzo as well as Zoot, the saxophone player, and Beauregard, the backstage assistant.

Probably the most famous character on the show other than Kermit was Miss Piggy, the chorus girl pig who was perpetually struggling toward stardom *and* who wanted to become Mrs. Kermit the Frog. No one could ever quite figure out how Miss Piggy became so successful. "No one creates a fad," Jim said. "It just happens. People love going along with the idea of a glamorous pig."

Frank Oz performed Piggy as well as Animal, Sam the Eagle, and lovable Fozzie the Bear, the funniest—and worst—stand-up comic in show biz, and also Kermit's best friend. Jerry Nelson was another main puppeteer for *The Muppet Show*. Among others, he performed a musician named Floyd, Kermit's nephew, Robin, and Dr. Strangepork, a mad scientist pig.

Many other puppeteers helped perform the huge cast. For the opening of the show a large Muppet audience had to be filmed. There were so many puppets in that scene that Jim called on every puppeteer he could find—not to mention stagehands, visitors, and janitors—each to hold a Muppet.

*The Muppet Show* was full of zany humor and lots of interesting creatures—a singing, guitar-playing watermelon patch, cowboy lobsters, and carrots singing opera. In fact, over 400 puppets were made for *The Muppet Show*!

As in all his other work, Jim made a point of using the Muppets to tell people about the things that he felt were important, like making peace and caring for our environment. One skit featured a woodland scene with animals singing and trying to hide from hunters. Another skit featured the entertainer Harry Belafonte singing a song about how people of different races should get along with one another.

Because there was a different guest star each week, the show was always fresh and exciting. Sometimes the guest star did what he or she was famous for doing: A singer might sing; a dancer might dance—or maybe not. Anything could happen. In one episode the cast came down with a mysterious illness, cluck-itis. It started with a penguin sneezing and suddenly turning into a chicken. Then other Muppets started sneezing and becoming chickens. The show ended with Kermit sneezing himself into a chicken. Fortunately his guest star, singer Roger Miller, told Kermit that it would wear off soon. Roger said he knew this because he'd had cluck-itis before!

In another episode, Brooke Shields was supposed to be Alice in Wonderland. Unfortunately the Muppets kept confusing Alice with Dorothy from the *Wizard of Oz*. The show ended with Brooke and the whole crazy cast singing "We're Off to See the Wizard." It wasn't *Alice in Wonderland* at all—it was Brooke in Muppetland!

"Some actors had a difficult time relating to the puppets as people," Jim observed. So he figured out a clever way to help make the guest stars feel more comfortable with the Muppets. Before filming began, the star had a meeting with Jim and the other puppeteers or writers. The guest would discuss what he or she wanted to do in the show. As the conversation went on, the Muppets would quietly join in. Soon the guest would forget that the Muppets weren't human. In fact, many guest stars were sad when the show was over because they couldn't go out for the evening with their new Muppet friends.

For a while, Jim had a hard time finding stars who were willing to appear on the show. He couldn't pay them very much, and a lot of actors didn't want to work with puppets. But as soon as the show became popular, it seemed as if everyone wanted to be on it. Some of the famous people who appeared on the show included Candice Bergen, George Burns, Bob Hope, Elton John, Steve Martin, Christopher Reeve, Peter Sellers, Sylvester Stallone, Lily Tomlin, Raquel Welch, and Orson Welles. During the show's second season Edgar Bergen (Candice Bergen's father and the ventriloquist whom Jim had listened to on the radio as a child) guest-starred, along with his "friend" Charlie McCarthy.

Once a week Jim and Frank would meet with the writers at a small Italian restaurant across the street from the studio to work on the script. Jerry Juhl was the head writer. The scripts were difficult to write because each one had to be full of fresh new humor. Jim would often respond to an idea he wasn't sure about by looking thoughtful and just saying, "Hmmmmm." Jim was never negative about an idea. But if he was unsure about it, he'd have the writers discuss it with him until eventually he was satisfied. Sometimes he drove everyone crazy because this could take a very long time, but Jim didn't stop working on an idea until he was completely happy with it.

On September 26, 1976, *The Muppet Show* aired for the first time in the United States on five CBS-owned television stations. By its third year on the air, the show was watched by more than 235 million people in over 100 countries around the world. From 1976 to 1981 *The Mup-*

*pet Show* won over a dozen different awards, including the 1978 Emmy Award for Outstanding Comedy-Variety or Music Series.

Pleased with the success of *The Muppet Show,* Lord Grade gave Jim the money he needed to make a full-length movie starring the Muppets. Jim dreamed of filming *The Muppet Movie* outside in the real world, though he knew it might be difficult. He saw it as another step toward making his puppets seem as lifelike as possible. In the opening scene of the movie, for example, Kermit sits in a lush swamp plucking a banjo and singing. The setting is beautiful and it looks totally natural, because it is real— Kermit was filmed on location in an actual swamp!

In fact, Jim operated Kermit from a small tank beneath the swamp's surface! A pump filled the tank with air, and Jim wore a diving suit. Through a sealed sleeve in the top of the tank Jim worked Kermit's head and the arm he used to strum his banjo. He watched how Kermit appeared to the camera on a video monitor inside the tank. Kermit's other hand, the one used to finger chords on the banjo, was performed by remote control by a technician on shore. A team of divers was on hand in case Jim got into trouble underwater.

Here, and throughout the film, Jim used new techniques to make it possible for the Muppets to do things they'd never done before. The result was a movie that seemed to make Kermit, Piggy, Fozzie, Gonzo, and the rest of the Muppet gang come to life effortlessly. All Jim's hard work paid off—he received plenty of praise when the movie was released in May 1979.

*The Muppet Show* and *The Muppet Movie* were both hits. So Lord Grade offered to help Jim make more movies. Jim could hardly wait to get started!

# Superstars

To the surprise of many people in the entertainment business, Jim decided to end production on *The Muppet Show* in 1980 at the height of its popularity. One hundred twenty episodes had been filmed. Jim had decided it would be better to end the show while it was still fun and exciting rather than wait until people got tired of it.

Thanks to the great success of *The Muppet Show,* Jim was able to move the New York offices of his company into a new building—kind of a Muppet Mansion. The "mansion" was actually an old townhouse on New York City's Upper East Side. The building housed the company's business offices, a publishing branch, designers' space, offices for Jim and his creative team, and a large workshop where puppets and model toys were made. Another workshop a few blocks away produced puppets on a larger scale.

The Muppets' new home was an unusual

office building. For one thing it was full of Muppets. Paintings of Muppets decorated the walls, and tiny Muppet figures perched on the desks and computers. Stunning handmade stained glass windows depicting Muppet characters immediately caught the eye of anyone walking by on the street. Even a Kermit the Frog telephone sat on a table in the reception area.

A beautiful spiral staircase wound through the building, connecting all four floors. Hanging from the center of the ceiling at the top of the staircase was a delicate hot air balloon sculpture decorated with tiny Muppet figures. Jim's son John worked as an assistant to the sculptor, John Kahn, who made this wonderful piece.

The workshop was overflowing with papers covered with sketches for new Muppets. It served as an experimental lab where new radio-controlled puppets were designed, built, and tested. Computer-operated puppets were dreamed up and brought to life there. The workshop also served as a hospital for Muppets in need of repair.

The office was always buzzing with people who were excited about working together on new projects. The Muppet Mansion reflected the same sense of lively fun that all of Jim's work did. It proved to be a good home for the Muppets.

Jim was not only working in New York *and* London, but his business trips took him all over the world. Work obligations made it difficult for Jim to spend time with his family, so he tried to bring them along with him whenever he could. By this time Lisa and Cheryl were both in college—and involved in their father's work. Jim loved to talk about his ideas with his children. He trusted them and was inspired by their young thinking. Lisa was talking with her father about some ideas she had for movies and a new show. Cheryl worked as Jim's assistant, a puppet-and-costume designer, and even as a puppeteer. She also talked about ideas with Jim. "We grew up in TV studios," Cheryl once said. "We all enjoyed being around Dad, and one of the best ways of being around him was to work with him—because when he was working he was always at his peak."

Brian was especially interested in puppeteering. John had become an apprentice to a sculptor. He was thinking about things he'd like to make films about someday. Heather was still young. But like the other Henson children she was exposed to the wonderful creative atmosphere of the Muppet family, and she was encouraged to develop her creative talents. She was soon inspiring the whole family.

As the children grew up, Jane began taking a more active role in the company again. As a vice president of HA! she was involved in the many complexities of the business. She was also very busy auditioning and training new puppeteers. Jane spent a lot of her time helping to encourage the young puppeteers and actors who performed the Muppets' characters in traveling live shows such as "Sesame Street on Ice" and "The Muppet Show Revue." These road shows were made by a different company, the VEE corporation. The regular puppeteers didn't have much time to spend on these shows. Jane enjoyed the exciting new way these shows brought the Muppets to life. She liked the idea of those big, live characters dancing and singing to children in their own towns.

These shows featured giant-size Muppet characters that sang and danced their way across the country. These live shows required special costumes and the usual attention to unusual details, like monster feet and shoes. One craftsperson was in charge of a small staff that just made shoes and feet for these crazy creations. A typical monster "foot" could weigh anywhere from 1½ to 3 pounds. The feet were made up of layers of surgical gauze, latex, and fake fur. One year over 90 pairs of feet were needed for the many road shows. And each pair of feet took almost 35 hours to create! The costume builders also had to come up with a light material that could be shaped into heads for these human-size Muppets. They ended up using a material called Kevlar, which is also used to make bulletproof vests!

In April of 1979 Kermit the Frog hosted the *Tonight* show. In 1980 Miss Piggy and Kermit appeared on the cover of *Life* magazine. All over the world Muppet toys, Muppet games, Muppet books, and even Muppet sheets, wallpaper, and dishes were being sold. It seemed as if the Muppets were everywhere. It was Muppet mania! In five short years, the Muppets had become international superstars.

Jim was now in charge of an empire of programs and products, and a growing staff in New York and London. He didn't have much time to relax, but even he had to take time out once in a while. Some of his favorite things to do were going to the movies, reading books, spending time with his children, and taking photographs. He also enjoyed skiing and playing tennis. Because he traveled so often, he sometimes found himself in exotic places where he could go for a camel ride, or ride in a hot air balloon! He also loved quiet boat trips.

One of the few ways that Jim really indulged himself was by collecting fancy cars. He had always loved them, and now that he could afford to have whatever he liked, he bought some really neat cars, like a Lotus, which is a very fast, expensive racing car. Jim kept the Kermit-green Lotus in England. Since most cars there are small and dark, the Kermit-green Lotus really stood out.

Jim shared his money and used it to help many people. He was active in Puppeteers of America and in UNIMA, an international puppeteers organization. In 1980 Jim, along with Burr Tillstrom and Bil Baird, helped bring together puppeteers from all over the world at a festival in Washington, D.C. It was an exciting and important event for American and foreign puppeteers.

Jim also created The Henson Foundation to award money to puppeteers nationwide who were doing innovative and unusual work in *adult* puppetry. With the money they received they were able to put on original shows. Jim wanted to teach people about the history and art of puppetry. So he sponsored a traveling art exhibit called "Art of the Muppets," about the Muppets, of course, and how they were made and how they worked. It included a display of the special materials used to create Muppet creatures. Jim made sure that the materials were displayed so that children could actually touch them.

Jim lived a calm life compared to many people in the entertainment business. He took care of his body by eating good food and staying away from cigarettes, drugs, and alcohol. He also exercised to stay in shape. Puppeteering is a physically demanding job, and it's important to stay strong and limber to be able to work the puppets for long stretches of time in uncomfortable positions. As Jim grew older he became more concerned with staying fit so that he would be able to continue his work.

People often asked Jim about the secret of his success. "Follow your enthusiasm," he replied. "It's something I've always believed in. Find those parts of your life you enjoy the most. Do what you enjoy doing."

# Fantastic Worlds

In 1981 the second Muppet movie, *The Great Muppet Caper,* was released. Jim not only wrote and performed in this film, he also directed it. This time Kermit and Fozzie play identical twin detectives—even though they don't look anything alike!—who are trying to solve the case of the stolen baseball diamond.

One of the most technically amazing scenes is the one in which Kermit, Miss Piggy, and other Muppets go bicycle riding through a park. On screen the Muppets seem very carefree, but the scene actually required hours of work, dozens of technicians, and years of experiments. The scene in which Kermit sings and dances around a room while dressing himself in a tuxedo was also very difficult to pull off. It took a lot of puppeteers to help Kermit just put on pants and a shirt!

The same crew that worked on *The Great Muppet Caper* also worked on Jim's third movie,

*The Dark Crystal.* Making *The Dark Crystal* gave Jim the chance to pursue his dream of being an experimental filmmaker. It's amazing that these two films, which are so completely different from each other, were made by the same group of people.

*The Dark Crystal* tells the tale of two young Gelflings who must mend a broken crystal in order to heal their world. The Gelflings, small fairylike creatures, work with the ancient Mystics and the homely little Pod-people in an effort to overcome the evil and corrupt Skeksis. The environment Jim imagined for these creatures was a desert planet with a lush, swamplike oasis, a primitive village for the Mystics, and a dark, forbidding castle for the evil Skeksis.

Building the puppets for *The Dark Crystal* was quite a challenge. New materials had to be developed. Complex hydraulic and electrical systems and robotics techniques had to be invented to make the creatures move less like puppets and more like humans. New techniques for performing were also necessary— many of the puppets needed three or more people to perform them. And Gelflings were carried to the castle of the Skeksis by giant winged creatures performed by puppeteers on stilts wearing skeletonlike costumes. "Operating the larger creatures was such a physical workout that we started training a team of performers eight or nine months before we began shooting, to get their bodies in shape," Jim said.

*The Dark Crystal* took about five years to make and cost around 20 million dollars. Jim codirected the film with Frank Oz. A man named Gary Kurtz, who had coproduced *Star Wars*, was the producer of *The Dark Crystal*. Although making this film was very hard work, Jim found it exciting. "I'd never done anything on this scale before," he told a reporter. "We had 80 plasterers making the environment sets. We'd shoot six or eight creatures at a time, each with a crew of operators. It felt like big-time moviemaking."

*The Dark Crystal* was released in 1982. Although it was praised for its amazing advances in special effects, the film did not receive the rave reviews that the Muppet movies had. Many people were surprised that it was so different from the movies that Jim had already done.

Jim, however, was pleased with his own work. He had once again changed puppetry in a fundamental way. "You always try to take the things you've done before and make them a little bit better," Jim said, describing the new advances he'd made while creating *The Dark Crystal.* "But in many ways I don't think of the film as puppetry. We used all kinds of techniques, including radio control and mechanical figures."

Two important things happened as a result of Jim's work on *The Dark Crystal.* The workshop that had created all the wonderful creatures and sets for the film became a business called The Creature Shop. The Creature Shop went on to create strange creatures and environments for other films that Jim was not producing himself, like the heroes of *Teenage Mutant Ninja Turtles.*

And many of the radio-control techniques used in *The Dark Crystal* were later applied in *Fraggle Rock,* Jim's new children's TV series that premiered in 1983 on HBO. The Fraggles were happy little creatures who liked to sing and have interesting adventures. Tiny creatures called Doozers lived in harmony with the Fraggles. The Gorgs were giants who weren't quite as easy to get along with. Jim wanted *Fraggle Rock* to be an entertaining show that promoted ideas about world peace. He felt it was very important that people learn to get along with one another.

"We're trying to do a nice show that has a reason for being," Jim explained. "There is a great need for quality children's programming, and I love to go into fresh places and create a world you can believe in." *Fraggle Rock* did accomplish that goal. The show won many awards for excellence. And, amazingly enough, on January 8, 1989, *Fraggle Rock* became the first American television series to be broadcast in the Soviet Union!

In June 1984, Jim's last Muppet movie, *The Muppets Take Manhattan,* was released. Frank Oz wrote and directed this film. The plot involves Kermit and his Muppet buddies who come to New York City to try to put a show on Broadway. It's a silly, wonderful movie with a happy ending. Like the two Muppet movies that came before it, it was successful.

Also in 1984 *Jim Henson's Muppet Babies* began airing. It was Jim's first Saturday morning cartoon show, and it won him more Emmy Awards! Jim had been interested in animation since his college days. The characters in the show used their imaginations to take wonderful adventures. Aside from regular cartoon drawings, the images seen in *Muppet Babies* included backdrops from all different kinds of real-life movies.

That year Jim also began work on another feature film called *Labyrinth,* the story of a young girl who wishes that the goblin king would take her crying baby brother away—and before she knows it, he does! She must then make her way through a maze called the Labyrinth, fight her way through the goblin city, and enter the goblin king's castle to rescue her little brother. The film spectacularly combines Muppets with live actors. The special effects include talking doorknobs that ask riddles and a knighted fox who rides a sheepdog. The goblins are scary, but there are also very Muppet-like creatures in *Labyrinth,* including a huge, gentle monster who befriends the young girl.

Jim was happy to be able to work with three of his children on this film. Jim, Lisa and Cheryl had discussed the concept for the film a great deal. Cheryl worked as a hand-puppet builder and performed one of the small creatures. Brian worked as the film's puppeteer coordinator. He also helped perform Hoggle, one of the puppets that helps the young girl complete her quest. He even did Hoggle's voice!

But not many people saw *Labyrinth* when it opened in 1986—and many who did see it didn't really like it. Jim was very disappointed that his audience didn't understand this film, because it meant a lot to him. It was unusual for Jim to be down, but this was a real lowpoint. "I think that was the closest I've seen him to turning in on himself and getting quite depressed," his son Brian explained. "It was a rather bad time, and he went to the south of France for a few days to wallow in it."

However, Jim didn't give himself much time to feel bad. He stayed busy constantly. "Many people think of work as something to avoid," Jim once said. "I think of work as something to seek."

Jim had become a very famous and wealthy man. He had houses in London, California, Florida, Connecticut, and New York City. These were comfortable homes, filled with beautiful things like handmade tables and chairs and Jim's collection of ancient artwork from all over the world. Jim also supported the work of craftsmen he admired by buying their work to decorate his homes. He was not flashy or greedy. Though these houses were lovely, they were also simple. Most important, having these homes gave Jim's five children a place to stay when they visited him.

By the mid-1980's Lisa was working for Warner Bros., the large film company. Cheryl had become interested in designing textiles, clothes, and costumes. Like his father, Brian had decided on a career as a puppeteer and filmmaker. John was an artist and film-maker. Heather, who was still in high school, was also showing an interest in art and animation.

The Hensons were a close family, but things had been hard for Jim and Jane because he was so busy traveling and working. So they decided not to live together anymore. It was a confusing time not only for them but for the whole family. It was also difficult for the company, since everyone had worked together so closely. Still, Jim and Jane remained friends.

In 1986 the Muppets celebrated thirty years of performing! By now Jim was traveling between offices in London, New York, and Toronto, Canada (where *Fraggle Rock* was ending production), as well as making appearances all over the world where fans gathered to hear him speak. Even though some of his projects were more popular than others, people everywhere looked forward to what might come next.

# New Directions

In 1987 Jim Henson received a well-deserved honor—he was inducted into the Television Academy Hall of Fame. His work had influenced puppetry, children's television, and movies all around the world.

Jim decided to start an awards program for young designers interested in puppetry. Artists, engineers, architects, and designers at art schools and universities all over the country were invited to enter a contest—they had to submit ideas for new Muppets. Jim and his staff of Muppet builders judged the entries. Five awards were given each year. The winners were not only given money but brought to New York to meet with Jim and the puppet builders in the Muppet workshop. Jim hoped his awards program would encourage young people to pursue puppetry.

Jim also began to work on a number of new projects. He had wanted to do a TV show about folk tales and fairy tales for a long time. He and his daughter Lisa talked a lot about this idea, and what they came up with was a new series called *The Storyteller.* The first episode of the series, a tale called "Hans: My Hedgehog," won an Emmy Award.

In 1988 Jim worked on a magical new film called *Witches,* directed by Nicholas Roeg. *Witches* tells the story of a little boy who gets turned into a mouse. The film has lots of scary characters. In some ways the creatures in it are like those in *Labyrinth* and *The Dark Crystal,* but the mouse itself is very realistic. The work was done at The Creature Shop in London.

The project nearly drove everyone crazy. "We had to build three scales of mice," Jim explained. "The mouse-size mouse, which we called the A mouse, was a tiny little thing with clockwork mechanisms. The B mouse was cable-controlled, and we did most of the film with him . . . the C mouse was a decent hand puppet. And his mouth was very expressive. It could be manipulated very well." A different set had to be built for each mouse. The crew had to figure out details like how long the mouse hair should be on each puppet so that they all looked totally realistic on the screen.

A short while later Jim worked with the makers of the film *Teenage Mutant Ninja Turtles,* who wanted his help in making the turtles look as real as possible. New advances made the movements of the turtles' mouths look almost lifelike. Jim's son Brian was one of the puppeteer directors on *Ninja Turtles.*

While crews in London were busy working on mice and turtles, crews in Toronto were busy producing a new TV series called *The Jim Henson Hour.* It was something like *The Muppet Show.* In this series Kermit is supposed to be in charge of a group of crazed Muppets who are trying to run a television station. *The Jim Henson Hour* premiered on NBC in 1989. Although the show received great reviews and won plenty of awards, it was canceled after only a few episodes. Once again, Jim was disappointed.

The 1980's had been a very creative period for Jim Henson. He had been able to create entire new universes. He had had some incredible successes and some disappointments. But he never stopped coming up with ideas. The problem was, he didn't always have time to develop his ideas.

In August 1989 Jim decided to sell the

Muppets to the Walt Disney Company. This meant that all the characters he had created (except for those on *Sesame Street*) would become part of the same company that ran Walt Disney World and Disneyland. The Muppets would join the same family as Mickey Mouse, Donald Duck, Bambi, and the Little Mermaid.

Jim's decision to sell his company came as a big surprise to everyone. When people asked him why he made this decision, he replied that he wanted to spend less time doing business. "I'll hope to spend a lot more of my time on the creative side of things," he said. Also, Jim felt sure that his work would be carried on into the future if the Muppets became part of the Disney family. Though he was not quite 53 years old, Jim was worried about what would happen to his creations when he retired or died. As it turned out, the deal didn't go through.

There remained lots of important things Jim wanted to do and say. He continued to fly all over the world to oversee his many projects and to keep in touch with his children. He still performed for *Sesame Street* because he felt that it was an important show that helped children. He began working on a new TV show to be called *Jim Henson's Mother Goose Stories*. He also wanted to create a new series that would help teach children (and adults) more about the environment and how to take good care of our earth. Jim had plans to do a mini-series based on the tale *Gulliver's Travels*. He also thought about doing a series of Greek myths. There was even talk of doing a live Broadway show featuring the Muppets.

The future seemed full of possibilities.

# It's a Good Life

Jim Henson died unexpectedly of pneumonia on May 16, 1990. His family and friends were shocked, as were the millions of people all over the world who had come to love him through his work. It was so sad to think that Jim's extraordinary spirit had left the world. In the middle of so many projects, so much activity, and so much promise for the future, Jim was suddenly gone.

Jim had hardly ever been sick. But shortly before his death he had come down with a cold. The cold didn't get better. In fact, Jim's illness turned out to be very serious.

The disease Jim had is usually cured by medicine called antibiotics. In recent years, however, a new strain of it has killed many people because it makes them sick so quickly. There isn't enough time to get the medicine sometimes. A milder form of this disease causes strep throat.

Jim waited to go to a doctor for many reasons. For one thing, he didn't believe that he was seriously ill. Also, he had been raised in a Christian Science household. Christian Scientists believe that you stay well by living according to God's laws. Prayer and meditation are often tried before medicine to heal an illness. But perhaps the most important reason why Jim didn't seek medical help was that he simply didn't want to cause anyone any trouble. He kept thinking he would feel better. He wanted to get back to work.

Jim spent the last hours of his life with Jane. When he realized he couldn't catch his breath and his heart was racing, Jim and Jane decided to go to the hospital. Sadly, by that time, Jim was too sick to be helped by the antibiotics he was given. His family and friends waited anxiously to hear if he was getting better. But within 24 hours he died.

Jim had made careful preparations for his death. A few years earlier, when he was on vacation in France after finishing his work on *Labyrinth,* he had written letters to each of his children full of loving advice and wisdom to be read after his death. One of the many memorable things he said in these letters revealed

Jim's own approach to life: "Please watch out for each other and love and forgive everybody. It's a good life, enjoy it."

He also asked his children not to be sad about his dying. "I suggest you first have a friendly little service of some kind," he wrote. "It would be lovely if there was a song or two . . . and someone said some nice happy words about me."

People found it hard to say good-bye to Jim Henson. The service arranged to celebrate Jim's life was overflowing with the love of thousands of people who filled the Cathedral of St. John the Divine in New York City. Jim had requested that no one wear black, only bright colors. People waved brilliant paper butterflies in the air. Big Bird sang "It's Not Easy Being Green" instead of Kermit. A bunch of silly clucking chicken Muppets also sang a song!

Many of the people Jim had worked with stood up before the crowd to tell stories about how fun it had been to work with Jim and be his friend. His wife and children talked about him, too. It was very sad that Jim was gone, but the ceremony itself was not really sad. It celebrated the amazing achievements Jim had left behind. At the beginning and at the end of the service, a Dixieland band played, just as Jim had requested.

Jim Henson once said that it was his goal in life to leave the world a better place than he had found it. "There was a quality that I could never quite grasp about Jim," Jane Henson told a reporter after Jim's death. "But he needed to accomplish something. He knew he could make a difference." There is no doubt that he managed to do that with his wonderful Muppets. But he also did it simply by being a truly great man. By the example of his own life he inspired many, many people to put their hearts into their work, to love life, and to be kind and generous.

"Dad was such a huge inspiration," his son Brian remembered. "My father had wonderful goals and wonderful dreams. And when he died, I realized they had become mine. And I saw that in virtually everyone in the company. So I think in some ways, he's still there in everyone."

Jim felt that death was a passage to another place where exciting things would happen. He expected to see his brother, Paul, his mother, and his friends who had died before him.

Wherever he was going, he expected to be doing some kind of interesting work. He had lived a life of wonder, and he had touched the world. But most important of all, he had done a good job.

*Highlights in the Life of*
**JIM HENSON**

**1936** James Maury Henson is born on September 24 in Leland, Mississippi.

**1951** Jim makes his first puppet.

**1954** Jim gets his first job, at WTOP in Washington, D.C.

**1955** *Sam and Friends* first airs on WRC-TV, Washington, D.C.'s NBC affiliate.
Jane Nebel joins *Sam and Friends*.

**1956** The Muppets appear on the *Tonight* show with Steve Allen.

**1958** Jim graduates from the University of Maryland and spends the summer in Europe.

**1959** *Sam and Friends* wins an Emmy Award for Best Local Entertainment Program.
Jane Nebel and Jim Henson marry.

**1960** Lisa Henson is born.
The Muppets move to New York City.

**1961** Muppets appear as regulars on *The Today Show* and the *Ed Sullivan Show*.
*Sam and Friends* ends.
Jerry Juhl joins the company.
Cheryl Henson is born.

**1963** Frank Oz and Don Sahlin join the company.
Muppets appear as regulars on the *Jimmy Dean Show*.
Brian Henson is born.

**1964** Jim makes a short film, *Timepiece*.

**1965** *Timepiece* receives an Academy Award nomination.
John Henson is born.

**1969** On November 11 the first episode of *Sesame Street* airs.

**1970** Heather Henson is born.

**1974** The Sesame Street Muppets win an Emmy Award for Outstanding Achievement in Children's Programming.

**1976**  On September 26 *The Muppet Show* first airs in the United States.

**1978**  *The Muppet Show* receives an Emmy for Outstanding Comedy-Variety or Music Series.

**1979**  *The Muppet Movie* opens.

**1980**  *The Muppet Show* ends production.

**1981**  *The Great Muppet Caper* opens.

**1982**  *The Dark Crystal* opens.

**1983**  *Fraggle Rock* first airs.

**1984**  *The Muppets Take Manhattan* opens.
*Jim Henson's Muppet Babies* first airs.

**1986**  *Labyrinth* opens.
*Fraggle Rock* ends production.

**1987**  Jim is inducted into the Television Academy Hall of Fame.

**1989**  *Fraggle Rock* becomes the first American TV show to air in the U.S.S.R.
*The Jim Henson Hour* first airs.

**1990** Jim Henson dies of pneumonia on May 16.

"Here Come the Muppets" opens at Walt Disney World's Disney MGM Studios Theme Park.

Nicholas Roeg's film *The Witches* opens.

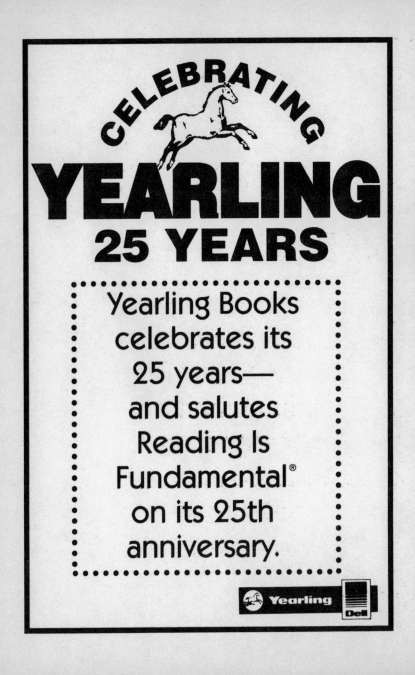

# FAMOUS PEOPLE...
# FAMOUS TIMES...
# FAMOUS PLACES!

*You'll find them all in the exciting new Yearling Biography series.*